IMAGES OF V

WITH THE GUNS
1914–1918

A SUBALTERN'S WAR

A 3in anti-aircraft gun photographed by Lieutenant Harold Cooper Bebington in 1918.

IMAGES OF WAR

WITH THE GUNS 1914–1918

A SUBALTERN'S WAR

RARE PHOTOGRAPHS FROM WARTIME ARCHIVES

Stanley Foxall and John Jones

Pen & Sword
MILITARY

First published in Great Britain in 2016 by
PEN & SWORD MILITARY
an imprint of
Pen & Sword Books Ltd,
47 Church Street,
Barnsley,
South Yorkshire
S70 2AS

A CIP record for this book is available from the British Library.

ISBN 978 147386 065 0

Typeset by CHIC GRAPHICS

Printed and bound by CPI Group (UK) Ltd, Croydon, CR0 4YY

Pen & Sword Books Ltd incorporates the imprints of Pen & Sword Archaeology,
Atlas, Aviation, Battleground, Discovery, Family History, History, Maritime, Military,
Naval, Politics, Railways, Select, Social History, Transport, True Crime, Claymore
Press, Frontline Books, Leo Cooper, Praetorian Press, Remember When, Seaforth
Publishing and Wharncliffe.

For a complete list of Pen & Sword titles please contact
Pen & Sword Books Limited
47 Church Street, Barnsley, South Yorkshire, S70 2AS, England
E-mail: enquiries@pen-and-sword.co.uk
Website: www.pen-and-sword.co.uk

Contents

Introduction

This story began, for the authors at least, in an auction house at Beeston in rural Cheshire. A number of First World War era photograph albums and other related items of militaria from the same source were going under the hammer. Interest was high, possibly because of the centenary of the start of the Great War, but by the end of the sale four albums of carefully mounted and annotated small photographic images produced from the type of pocket camera available at that time, together with a pair of broken spurs, regimental badges on a horse girth strap, a hip flask and Royal Artillery cap badges were in the authors' possession as their new custodians.

On careful inspection, it was found that the albums documented one man's Great War experiences in pictures from his training and later recovery after being wounded. Additionally, what was initially thought to be a uniform study transpired to be those postcard pictures so popular at the time which showed his relatives, friends and work colleagues in uniform as they set off in the earlier years of the War to 'do their bit' for King and Country.

Further research on the albums identified the photographer as Harold Cooper Bebington, a man who lived in Liscard, Wallasey, then in the County of Cheshire, with a family business located in Liverpool. This is his Great War story and, in part, those of his friends and his company's employees that have been identified from his annotations and as told by his pictures.

Sources and Acknowledgements

Commonwealth War Graves Commission.
National Archives UK.
Wallasey Central Library – Reference Library.
www.historyofwallasey.co.uk
Wallasey Heritage Centre.
Actual copies of *The Times* and the *Daily Mirror* from the First World War period.
Numerous divisional/regimental histories by Major C. H. Dudley Ward.

Farndale, General Sir Martin, *The History of the Royal Regiment of Artillery*, London, 1986.
Graves, Robert, *Good-Bye to All That*, The Folio Society, London, 1981.
Hogg, Ian V., *The Guns 1914-18*, Pan/Ballantine, London, 1973.
Holmes, Richard, *Shots from the Front*, Harper Press, London, 2010.
McGilchrist, A. M., *The Liverpool Scottish 1900-1919*, Henry Young and Sons Ltd, Liverpool, 1930.
Richards, Frank, *Old Soldier Sahib*, Naval and Military Press Ltd, Uckfield, reprint of 1933 edition.

Chapter One

The Photographer

Harold Cooper Bebington was born on 31 October 1892 in Liscard, part of Wallasey on the Wirral peninsula situated between the Victorian seaside town of New Brighton and the Mersey ferry port of Seacombe. His home at Marine Terrace, a property which still exists today, overlooked the River Mersey and the then very busy shipping trade of the Liverpool waterfront (Liverpool has been referred to as the second city of the Empire). He was the youngest son of Alfred and Jessie Selina Bebington, his brothers and sister being Alfred (18 at the time of Harold's birth), Florence (17) and Charles (12), so he was very much a younger addition to the family. The family were food importers and Wholesale Provisions Merchants running a business called Thomas Peate and Company with premises (including a smokehouse) in Liverpool, the offices being at 14 and 16 Richmond Street, Whitechapel, then in the heart of the thriving commercial district. The company was a member of the Liverpool Provision Trade Association founded in 1874 which encouraged overseas trading and covered all imported pig and dairy produce, eggs and canned goods etc. The Association's exchange provided a 'trading floor' and in 1912 it added a lard futures market. By the time of the 1911 census however, father Alfred was dead and only Harold remained at home living with his mother at 10 Marine Terrace. Elder brother Charles was working in the family business as a salesman but living in Liverpool.

Harold's home at Marine Terrace is close to an area of Wallasey called the Magazine where in the past gunpowder from sailing ships was stored to protect the port and city of Liverpool from damage by accidental explosion. As a boy, Harold would have played with local friends such as Wack (of whom more later) on Magazine Parade on the banks of the River Mersey and in the old Fort area where at that time obsolete gun barrels still remained and which may have influenced his later decision to join the Royal Artillery.

Harold had an interest in photography, and for some time was a member of the Wallasey Amateur Photographic Society. Advances in the early twentieth century meant that the developing of pictures could take place in daylight in an ordinary room. Small pocket cameras appeared, manufactured by both the American

Present-day view of Marine Terrace.

Children playing football outside the old Fort in the early 1900s. Note the gun barrel and its carriage abandoned adjacent to the wall of the Fort.

Locals at the Fort circa 1910.

Liscard High School for Boys,

Hale Road and Seabank Road, Liscard.

Head Master—Mr. A. WRIGLEY, B.A. Lond

A Highly Successful School.

Thorough Individual Attention.

Large Playing Field near the School.

PROSPECTUS ON APPLICATION.

As the youngest son, Harold benefited from the then well-established family business and affluence, and was educated privately at Liscard High School for Boys.

company Kodak (the Vest Pocket Kodak – VPK) and a British company called Houghtons Limited, and with the outbreak of the First World War in August 1914 many of these cameras were purchased and taken abroad by members the British Expeditionary Force (BEF). These cameras were not cheap at the time, costing in the order of 30 shillings, and only produced small images but they were a 'must have' item for the committed enthusiast.

The spread of these cameras and the subsequent selling by soldiers of such photographs to the Press, who were anxious for war news 'scoops', resulted in the Commander-in-Chief of the BEF issuing General Routine Order Number 464 prohibiting the taking of photographs. A further order issued on 16 March 1915 stated that photographic cameras were not allowed to be in the possession of Officers, Non-Commissioned Officers or men whilst serving with the British Army in the Field. Harold was later to ignore this.

With a business in Liverpool, Harold would have used the regular ferry service to travel from his Wirral home across the River Mersey through the bustling shipping lanes to the city and back on a daily basis. The ferry boats in use included the *Daffodil* and *Iris II*, both of which were to play significant parts in the Royal Navy raid on Zeebrugge in April 1918.

Many of Harold's relatives and friends joined the Colours at the outbreak of war in 1914; it was still voluntary at this stage since conscription was not brought in until January 1916. He will also have registered under the Derby Scheme, named after Lord Derby, in the summer of 1915 for potential recruitment, but Harold working in the food industry could well have justified an exemption. However as early as 1915 it is clear he was already considering how to serve his Country. A family friend, Lieutenant-Colonel Archibald Gordon Gullan of the Royal Army Medical Corps (RAMC) – Territorial Force, may have advised him of the course of action to take to join as a commissioned officer. Harold applied for a commission in the Territorial Force in early October 1915 on Army Form E.536, passed a medical, and gained a first reference from his sponsor Colonel Gullan, by then RAMC Territorial Force officer commanding 1/3 West Lancashire Field Ambulance based at Canterbury. Gullan stated 'I hereby certify to the good moral character of Harold C Bebington whom I have known for the last six years'. More of him later.

In February 1916 Harold was staying at Maxells Hotel in the Strand, London, having completed the University of London Officer Training Corps course which had lasted for four months. These Officer Training Corps (OTCs) in the Universities ran courses of instruction in order to train officers for the Army. During these courses, the students were quartered in the University and had use of its grounds and of any lecture theatres required for the tuition aspects of the course. In February 1916, however, the War Office changed the regulations governing the selection of officers, and all from then on all candidates had to pass through an Officers' Cadet Battalion undertaking a course of instruction which lasted for five months, entirely separate from the OTCs. Hence, from this time on, there was an understandable decline in numbers of prospective officers attending University OTCs across Britain. Harold may well have been amongst the last of those to choose to follow the OTC route to a commission.

A subsequent reference on his Army Form E.536 dated 19 February 1916 from the University of London OTC's commanding officer seems to have completed the suitability part of the application process, and with an 'Imperial and General Service Obligation' to allow Territorial Force members to serve overseas signed by Harold on 22 February (originally the Territorial Force had been raised for home service only and had not been regarded by Kitchener as being suitable as part of the Army in the field, although he was to be proved wrong). A Short Service Attestation form was completed at Exeter on 31 March and Harold became 150151 Gunner Harold Cooper Bebington of the Royal Regiment of Artillery. The five-month officer training as a Cadet of Gunner Bebington had begun, and with him went his camera.

Chapter Two

The Training of an Artillery Officer

During the First World War, the Royal Horse and Field Artillery training establishments were located at:

Artillery Reception Brigade   Officer training, Brighton
Number 1 Officer Cadet School   St John's Wood
Number 2 Officer Cadet School   Exeter
Number 3 Officer Cadet School   Weedon
Signalling Training School   Crowborough
Gunnery School   Chapperton Down, Larkhill

Gunner Bebington was allocated to the 18th Reserve Battery of the Royal Field Artillery at Topsham Barracks in the city of Exeter, which was also the home of 16th and 17th Batteries of 3B Reserve Brigade.

The officer commanding 18th Reserve Battery Royal Field Artillery at Topsham Royal Artillery Cadet School at this time was Major Arthur Rice Knox. Born in 1863, the son of Major General T. Knox also of the Royal Artillery (RA), and entering the RA in 1883, he was a distinguished veteran of the Boer War where he had been involved in actions such as the Relief of Ladysmith and the action at Spion Kop. Mentioned in despatches and awarded the Distinguished Service Order (DSO), he had been retired in 1908 but called back into military service. Perhaps of particular assistance to Bebington was the fact that Knox himself was interested in photography, having taken photographs of his Army service in India in 1898, and this may have resulted in many of the following photographs having being allowed to be taken at all!

1916 – Cadet Bebington (the photographer) at Teignmouth on a Douglas motorcycle. He has spent time and money on his appearance; there is evidence of tailoring in the breeches, reinforcement to the puttees and he is wearing officers' leather gloves (standard military-issue gloves of the time were of wool). Note the spurs on his boots! The white cap band indicates his Cadet status, he has a moustache as was standard for the British Army of this time and a well-polished 1903 pattern bandolier. On his wrist is a watch. Throughout most of the War the timepieces officially issued to British military officers were pocket watches; officers were expected to supply much of their own kit, including a wristwatch if they wanted one. It was only towards the end of the war in 1917 that the War Office started considering wristwatches. As Cadet Bebington is still ranked as a Gunner at this time, he must have purchased the watch himself.

Two new cadet friends trying out the same Douglas motorcycle. The cadet in the front is wearing a raincoat, probably a Burberry (still available to purchase today). The cadet at the back is seated on the pannier, this particular Douglas model having only one seat. Motorcycles were requisitioned for military use as were horses and London buses. During the First World War the Douglas company was a major manufacturer and supplier to the military, supplying in excess of 60,000 motorcycles.

'Lunchtime doze.' Harold Cooper Bebington, officer cadet Royal Regiment of Artillery (RA). Here he is seemingly dozing at Exeter, but still guarding the blankets that are airing in the sun. As any old soldier can tell, if it's not nailed down it will walk!

Cadet 'Abe', one of Bebington's closer friends, admiring the sea view at Teignmouth. He is a Bombardier in the RA and wears a form of trenchcoat not normally issued to other ranks, perhaps also indicating a privileged background. See also the spurs.

'Guard fall in', Exeter. Smartly-dressed non-commissioned officer (NCO) instructors and Gunners on parade. Note that there are only three rifles present on the parade; the RA followed an issue of firearms to men ratio (approximately one rifle for four men) that dated from 1814 and lasted until the Second World Wa,r which frequently left gunners defenceless in the event of infantry assault. In Crete in 1941, for example, gunners were overrun, being unable to defend themselves and their guns due to lack of firearms, which led to the loss of the airfield and eventually Crete itself.

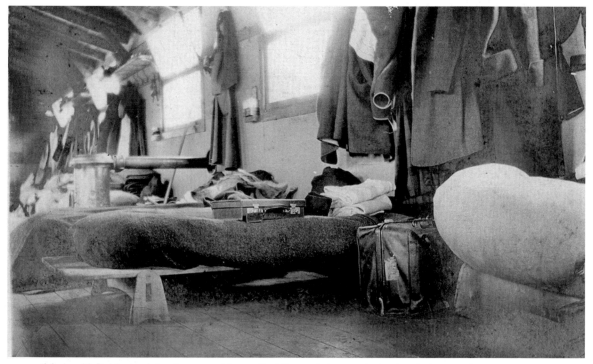

'My bunk'. Bebington's bedspace, evidence that the cadets were being treated as gentlemen – an infantry barracks would have been squared away each morning. Note the quality of the luggage, and his bed being next but one to the heater – a prime position; much clutter, the bane of sergeant-majors everywhere! The other ranks' bed in the foreground is rolled as stored. All clothes are hanging up on pegs; no lockers in those days.

Teignmouth.

The Work Begins

'Out with the teams, Exeter.' Horsepower in its literal sense was the moving force for the Royal Field Artillery, into which Bebington was training to be commissioned. Here the team with a full crew of six is towing an ammunition wagon which would have carried thirty-eight rounds. If he could not already ride, Bebington would have undergone a short course of instruction under a Royal Artillery riding master so that he would at least be a competent rider. The gun teams moved at speed, and an officer would be expected to lead the way.

A team of six horses with cadet riders at the trot under the supervision of another cadet acting as an NCO. The control of the horses, gun and limber, together weighing several tons, required each member to perform their duties as part of a team effort to achieve maximum military efficiency. Each cadet would learn each job within the team, the requirement for potential officers. Of note are the docked horse's tails and hogged manes, standard military procedure of the time.

'Out with the teams, Woodbury.' Woodbury is a village in East Devon some seven miles south-east of Exeter, so the cadets under instruction are now able to take the teams further afield. The picture shows a break in training, but care of the horses took precedence over that of the men – no horse, no gun! Here the horse, tack and limber are all being inspected by the officer cadets. The Royal Artillery has always had high standards for its animal husbandry. Note the leg protection worn by the nearest cadet to prevent injury from the horses coming together, and his short greatcoat.

Woodbury village again, full gun teams at rest with local children watching on with interest. A soldier checks the hoof of his mount, watched by the fiercest critic – the small boy who would no doubt see service in the Second World War! Note the field guns in the background.

'Field day, Woodbury.' A rest break in field training. Of interest is the use of camouflage through the bushes.

'Corporal Hall.' Bombardier Hall. With his rank as an NCO, one can speculate that he has some service experience, perhaps even having fought in France. The teams with limbers and guns can be seen in line in the background.

'Lunchtime, Woodbury.' Feeding the horses. A good view of a docked horse's tail in the foreground. Whilst the cadets talk, note the proximity of a small boy to a large horse.

Cadet Bebington in full field gear comprising 1903 leather equipment, fifty-round bandolier, water-bottle and haversack, the latter which somewhat constricted the wearer's chest movement. It was still in use in the Second World War by mounted units. No provision for a bayonet as little thought was given to gunners' self-defence, the field gun being their weapon.

'Sergeant Bishop.' Battery Sergeant Major Bishop, instructor. A veteran perhaps of colonial campaigns, immaculately turned-out, wise to all schemes a gunner might try, the man who made a gunner out of the Cadet Bebington. Note the length of his riding crop. BSM Bishop also served in France and was awarded the Meritorious Service Medal for devotion to duty in 1918.

'Route march.' The guns on a route march, NCO to the left of picture riding at ease. The cadet gunners appear to be smoking whilst a civilian horse and cart passes by. The fields of Flanders seem so far away!

Cadet Bebington, a man in his prime, wearing full uniform, and officer's gloves complete with a Royal Artillery swagger stick designed to stop soldiers putting their hands in their pockets! His good nature is apparent in this relaxed photograph.

'Corporal Freeman. Abe.' Cadet Bombardier Abe Freeman, again in full uniform also with officer's gloves and swagger stick. Abe was obviously a good friend of Bebington's.

'The Reception. Sunday morning, Exeter.' Officer cadets at a later stage of training, a mixture of officer's uniform and gunner's gear in a state of 'undress'. A relaxed composition with a lady present. Discipline was harsh for other ranks, and females in barracks would have been against regulations. Only one regiment, the Norfolks, was allowed to have a lady present in barracks and she was Brittania on their cap badge! However, officer cadets were treated as gentlemen so different standards apply, it would seem. Bebington's ability as a photographer to get his subjects to relax adds to the wonderful nature of this picture. One cadet appears to be levitating!.

'Abe off to Okey'. Cadet Bombardier Abe Freeman off to Okehampton to enjoy some no doubt well-earned rest and recreation (r and r). Immaculately turned out as ever, he is carrying a riding crop without which he would be improperly dressed. Envious cadets look on as he boards the carriage. Note the civilian in white behind the back wheels of the cab – the local milkman perhaps?

A pre-war picture postcard view of Okehampton, Abe's destination for the day, showing its rural location.

'Summerlands.' Perhaps at a guest house with his mother, Jessie, Bebington is further advanced on his way to a commission indicated by an officer's uniform with tie but still with the white hat band indicating his continued cadet status. It took until 1944 for other ranks in the Army to be granted the privilege of wearing a tie.

Two officer cadets 'walking out' with a lady. The cadet on the left of the picture is in an other-ranks tunic, the one on the right in officer's service dress, both with swagger sticks. There are no indicators of previous service on their uniforms, i.e. no wound stripes or overseas chevrons. Puttees are worn by both, another item of kit derived from Indian service (along with cholera belts and spine pads to stop the spine melting!); puttees could also restrict the flow of blood to the feet and contribute to trench foot. In a later interview, a Second World War tank NCO and former 1930s boy soldier turned the air blue with his observations on puttees!

'Cadet McDonald.' A smart, well-built young man. Hopefully he survived his service with the guns.

Bombardier Abe Freeman and child taken in the garden of his home. This, no doubt, is what he knew he was fighting for. Leave was infrequent and prone to cancellation, so time spent at home with kith and kin was to be treasured.

Cadets' map-reading exercise. A most important aspect of the gunner's trade is being able to understand what to fire at! It is amazing to see the almost leisurely manner in which some aspects of the cadets' training are undertaken. Another well-posed picture taken by Cadet Bebington. The leeway given in their dress would no doubt have driven the Battery Sergeant Major almost to apoplexy. It can hardly be said that this training is taking place under 'service' conditions. Notice also the lack of essential combat equipment such as Brodie steel helmets, respirators or webbing; no doubt to be issued once on active service.

'Stonehenge.' Salisbury Plain, home of the British army and an artillery practice area from the Napoleonic Wars to the present day. In this picture Cadet Bebington as a tourist, a man of science and modern in his ways no doubt tipped his cap to our ancestors. The more recent fence is perhaps to keep away training soldiers who would like to leave their initials maybe?

'My bunk.' The soldier as an artist! Second Lieutenant Bebington's quarters. No longer subject to inspections as would be one of the other ranks, here we see a fashionable young lady drawn on the wall with the inscription 'In Amsterdam there lives a maid' which comes from a traditional but somewhat bawdy sea shanty, not very officer-like! Note how sparse the accommodation is but with a rug on the floor, a chest of drawers (rather battered perhaps due to incessant use by the officers in training passing through), polished boots in a neat row – and slippers. By now Bebington would have the services of a batman, so all that dreary polishing could be left to another as he concentrates on becoming proficient in the command of a section of two 18-pounder quick-firing field guns.

'Around and about Larkhill'. Officer cadets, Royal Regiment of Artillery on manoeuvres in the vicinity of Larkhill. They are individually mounted as they have mastered the team management stage. Note that the cadets are now wearing officer's uniform as seen by shirt and tie, no longer 'other ranks' 1903 pattern equipment. Although this picture was taken in 1916, the countryside is still at peace with no air of urgency obvious in either location nor indeed in the officer cadets, no field gear in evidence, all in all quite leisurely . . .

Mounted and dismounted officer cadets, some still wearing OR dress showing various stages of training. In France at this time the British Army is engaged in the Battle of the Somme, casualties already heavy and infantry units reformed time and again, yet apparently oblivious to all of this the Royal Artillery officer training goes about its business in a pre-war manner, producing well-trained cadets with horses in peak condition. It is thought that Bebington had little riding experience before the war, yet he had to develop his riding to a high standard as the guns when in action moved at speed, and a 'firm' seat was obligatory!

A lunch break for both man and horse. The horses would have been the officers 'charger' as opposed to the Australian 'whaler' used to such success by the Anzacs in Palestine.

A fine study of a section of 18-pounder guns and their ammunition wagons on exercise around Larkhill. The guns are operated as a pair. The men are constantly inspecting and checking both horses and equipment, any deficiencies would soon become apparent. For want of a nail the shoe was lost, as the French military proverb says . . .

Observation post, near Okehampton, though what use a dozen-plus officer cadets on a tor would be for all to see and snipe at one can only guess. Although the Army had been at war since August 1914, it was still slow to adapt tactically and still suffered from some pre-war doctrine. It should be borne in mind that the campaign on the Western Front, where most of these cadets were to serve, was one of entrenchment and concealment. To be seen was to give away your position, drawing down counter-battery fire from the enemy. Standing orders for artillery outposts in March 1918 have such useful warnings as beware the enemy can hear you, and that a (single) rifle should be provided – indicating that it was not standard issue for each gunner. By then, the Royal Artillery was the most efficient branch of the Army; it was innovative in use of all types of guns and more than a match for its opponents. The weight of fire that the Artillery could bring to bear by then was awesome, German reports confirming its ferocity. Gunnery officers learnt much from active service and applied that knowledge well. Lieutenant Bebington was to be serving in a new type of artillery by 1918, though.

As these gunners train in summer 1916, the Battle of the Somme continues to be fought and Kitchener's New Army was being destroyed by the Kaiser's army.

'Rangefinding'. Cadets using a rangefinder, with Cadet Bebington in shirtsleeve order with field glasses in centre of the picture. This picture could have been taken in India! A stone sangar has been constructed as seen in the right of the picture; no attempt has been made to camouflage the observer's position, exposed for all to see, no allowance for potential snipers or enemy artillery – it really is training for a gentleman's war so far. This is the army that having withdrawn the lance, from bitter experiences in the Boer War, reintroduced it as a fighting weapon in 1909 and forgets much of the practical experience it gained in that war, such as officers to dress like other ranks and swords to be left in storage. Field Marshal Montgomery later wrote that in 1914 on the outbreak of the war in August, standing orders were for officers to take their swords for sharpening! Robert Graves, the war poet and officer in the Royal Welch Fusiliers, wrote that after being seriously wounded and his pistol being stolen in the hospital, he never bothered to replace it, instead drawing a rifle and making use of that for the rest of his service.

'Observing'. A close-up shot of a rangefinder, moors in the background, with Cadet Bebington, in flagrant breach of standing orders, giving us a fine study of this secret piece of artillery equipment. In the centre of the picture, background, can be seen a soldier observing using field glasses from behind the cover of a large rock – fieldcraft in operation at last?

'Map-reading'. Another fine study of the officer cadets as they learn the complexities of map-reading, another essential skill for the gunnery officer. The cadets are again in varying states of dress, with tunic and shirt-sleeve order, and cigarettes – Tommy for the use of – in evidence.

'Directors. Larkhill.' The cadets are dressed in fatigues, probably the standard-issue cotton type, with each cadet carrying parts of the complicated directors. All the parts are in protective cases, presumably just issued to the cadets.

'On the Moors.' Back on Dartmoor in the vicinity of Okehampton, officer cadets refresh and amuse themselves in a stream.

'Cadet Nicholson'. One of Bebington's colleagues in shirtsleeve order next to a field glasses case. Bebington obviously enjoyed taking photographs of those he served with, and in this relaxed study the young soldier who is the subject rests in the sun, no doubt wondering what the future may bring.

'Yes Tor.' The highest peak in Devonshire, Yes Tor is about five miles from the town of Okehampton and rises to a height of upwards of 2,000 feet. In this picture the cadets are consolidating their map-reading skills. Note the pipe-smoking cadet with the short haircut also on view – this was a gesture towards vermin control sadly only being partially successful, lice being a nuisance to the average trench dweller!

'Off to Okey'. Six officer cadets of the Royal Artillery off to Okehampton. All are dressed in officer's service dress as opposed to the 1902 pattern tunic worn by other ranks, so being commissioned can't be far away. It was the silhouette of the British officer which made him so appealing to the enemy sniper, be he German, Turk or Austrian – the riding breeches together with the voluminous pockets created a hard to miss profile. 'Shoot the man with the thin knees!' Later in the War, even Guards officers dressed like other ranks and wore 1908 webbing. Instructions as early as 1915 instructed officers to dress like their men, but sadly it took time for it to become common practice. Anzac officers quickly followed this instruction in the Gallipoli campaign, perhaps being less hidebound than their British cousins.

Wagon train on the road from Amesbury to Larkhill, Salisbury Plain. Perhaps the officer cadets were wise in taking the train from Amesbury as seen in the preceding photograph! The main mover of equipment, arms and ammunition for the British Army was the General Service (GS) Wagon. This was partially superseded by the motor lorry during the War, but was still vital in keeping the army in the field and ready to fight. To the right of the picture, a young civilian is being given a ride. Whilst officially frowned upon, the majority of soldiers being 'hostilities only' no doubt would not see a youngster trapped by the rising waters. The reverse of the card reveals that the writer has just attended a Sunday Church Parade with 2,000 others, that he is 'alive and kicking' yet knows that he is departing for the Front within the week.

Whilst Bebington seems to have enjoyed uncommonly good weather for his officer training course as he passed down these same lanes with his 18-pounder gun teams at speed, this picture shows the reality at its worst. Not only are there floods to contend with by the team of waggoners, but the extra work created cleaning and maintaining wagons and the care of the horses cut into the already sparse free time of the rankers.

The war in Flanders was one of frequently inclement weather: rain was seldom appreciated as it never stopped the fighting and of course helped to create mud in a churned-up landscape. Dense, cloying, incapacitating mud into which guns could sink and the wounded drown, perhaps the one unifying item that spared neither side!

'Cadet Heaton' in a relaxed pose in service dress with cane and puttees, probably taken in Okehampton itself.

'Batmen, Larkhill.' Batmen were the officers' allocated servant, upon whom the officer cadets relied upon to maintain their high standard of turnout. In a large camp such as Larkhill where the photographer tells us this picture was taken, the batmen (all experienced Other Ranks soldiers) would probably have more than one 'gentleman' to take care of; maybe a life cleaning boots, polishing leather and pressing uniforms was preferable to the gun lines in France. The soldier at the back has two good conduct badges on display on his sleeve, whilst all three wear lanyards. The soldiers on the left and right wear the white lanyard of the Royal Artillery, the one in the middle has one of a darker colour. We can speculate that these older soldiers may be recuperating from wounds or other disabilities.

'Hut 15. Dinner Time, Topsham.' After a no-doubt adequate meal, the cadets relax. A cadet to the right of Hut 15 is wearing a version of the cap comforter rather than his service cap, whilst one seated at the door of the hut is enjoying his pipe. Soon it will be service-issue rations delivered (if at all) in a sack, consisting of tea leaves, bacon, cheese, bread and biscuit all mixed up, brought to the gun line by harassed Army Service Corps personnel. If fortunate, this could be eked out with parcels from home, perhaps from Harrods, perhaps from mother.

Humour is a strong element in some of Bebington's photography, and here cadets lark about in the gun lines. We can only speculate what is being worn under the service cap by the running gunner perhaps emulating a spotter aircraft and its pilot? The guns are in a firing line, 'ready' ammunition in place so the cadets are at that stage in their training when they are about to fire. An element of excitement may be permitted as they finally see all their training lead to live firing.

The Guns

'God fights on the side with the best Artillery . . . (Napoleon Bonaparte)

The 18-pounder field gun entered service with the Royal Regiment of Artillery in 1904. Its shell actually weighed 18.5lbs (8.4kg), in comparison with the French 75mm shell which weighed 6.2kg and the German 77mm shell weighing 6.85kg. Hence, potentially a British barrage carried considerably more weight than its opposite numbers. However, the number of dud or defective shells supplied to the British army (some still lying dormant in Flanders fields and creating a hazard for modern day French and Belgian farmers) reduced efficiency somewhat. The potentially dangerous Number 100 fuze was succeeded with Numbers 101, 102 and 103 which were still less than perfect for the job in hand. Things improved with the introduction of the Number 106 fuze based on French technology. Finally the Royal Artillery had a fuze which allowed a shell to explode on impact, useful for cutting barbed-wire entanglements, as opposed to the earlier fuzes which tended to bury themselves in the ground before detonating, creating a shell hole which could be an impediment to the infantry's advance. By the time Lieutenant Bebington was commissioned in 1916, the 18-pounder was equipped with three types of shell, smoke, high explosive and shrapnel. Later these would be joined by gas and incendiary rounds. During the Great War, some 99,300,000 18-pounder shells were fired on the Western Front alone!

Bebington was also fortunate that by 1916 there were sufficient numbers of 18-pounder guns to replace the obsolete 15-pounders with which the Territorial Force artillery was equipped at the beginning of the War. It is a very well-trained gunner subaltern that will shortly make his way to France.

A team of gunners with a shell pose for this photograph. In the background a second gun is being brought into position. Bebington no doubt is his role as section commander took advantage of his rank to take this well composed picture.

'Firing, Okehampton.' The picture shows an officer cadet detachment, one of whom could be Cadet Bebington, firing the gun in training. Note the long recoil of the gun barrel, an obvious hazard to a careless or tired gunner. The crew are stripped to shirtsleeve order and one has turned his cap back to front, a practice not seen in action. The round used would have a reduced charge, which would limit wear on the gun's barrel hence extending its life as a training weapon. The model of 18-pounder in use here would appear to be the Mark 2.

The gun's ammunition wagon is beside it, and the other gun of the section is in action a short distance away. Note the dust raised by firing; although this shot is training under combat conditions there is no evidence of anti-gas precautions and no attempt has been made to disguise the gun's location.

The gun and its crew in action. The savage 40-inch recoil of the piece can be seen, the crew operating efficiently with caution to avoid it. Gunners have ready rounds to feed the gun, which has a rate of fire of up to twenty rounds per minute although sustained fire was usually at the rate of four rounds per minute. The 18-pounder field gun as deployed in this picture had a range of 6,525 yards, but if a pit was dug for the trail of the gun, hence elevating its barrel, this increased to 7,800 yards. This gun weighed 1.282 tonnes and required a strong crew of ten as it was manhandled into action.

Once deployed to France, the gunners would be further trained in the 'gas schools' maintained by each division. Camouflage was also being developed as an art form, not just of the guns themselves but also for the gun positions using wire, wood and Hessian 'scrim'.

Another photograph of the 18-pounder in action. The five gunners, again in shirtsleeve order, attend to their individual roles. The NCO keeps his hand on the traversing lever, ready to alter direction if so ordered. The ammunition wagon is placed immediately to hand. Again, dust and smoke caused by firing gives away the gun's position. In France this would call down counter-battery fire upon them from the enemy, so a crucial lesson of artillery warfare was learnt – hit hard, hit fast. Note the gun shield which was designed to provide a modicum of protection for the gunners as they plied their deadly craft. Of interest is the unmanned signalling/observation post to the left of the gun. As has been mentioned previously, no evidence of rifles for the defence of the guns is evident.

While 'freshly minted' subalterns train in dry conditions in Blighty in summer 1916, the Royal Regiment of Artillery is fighting in the battle of the Somme at great cost in men and materials. Their turn will come soon!

Battery Sergeant Major Bishop has obviously made his presence felt as spent shell cases have been collected and neatly stacked as can be seen when compared to the previous photographs. Sergeant majors do so love a tidy battlefield!

The 18-pounder was still in service with the British army in 1940, though by then as the Mark 4 model and largely in a training role, but it was to serve the Irish Defence Force until the 1970s, a long lifespan for a good gun.

Relaxed officer cadets ponder the discipline of map reading. In the forefront is a regular NCO, recognisable by his lack of white cadet hatband; also of note is his use of leather leggings, a far more comfortable option to puttees. The cadet to the right of centre seems to be wearing a knotted handkerchief on his head – sartorial elegance or Bond Street latest maybe?

Nearly there . . .end of training in sight. A quietly content, soon to be subaltern, Bebington. Sam Browne waist belt now being worn, with long boots and pale riding breeches. Perhaps on arriving in France a lesson on what to wear in the trenches will be given, though perhaps the Royal Artillery put style before practicality?

Cadet Bebington at his leisure, making himself at home in a field. The sun shines, a packed lunch in evidence and a batman to do the ironing! Only a fool experiences discomfort when there is comfort to be had. Oh what a lovely war . . . so far!

The Accommodation

Barrack room. As a potential officer/gentleman, Bebington is able to indulge his artistic inclinations. He appears to be a talented artist, his chosen subject being the fair female. The accommodation although sparse, is far from the Spartan accommodation of the other ranks. Chairs appear comfortable, even though a deck chair seems to have been pressed into military use. Here at least a cadet could study in privacy, maybe the most valuable commodity.

Another view of the barrack room. The bed has adequate blankets, and although no sign of any heating the well-made structure of the hut should be noted. Some similar huts sold from the Goch prison camp in North Wales after the War were still in use in local gardens in the Bala area some 100 years after they were built!

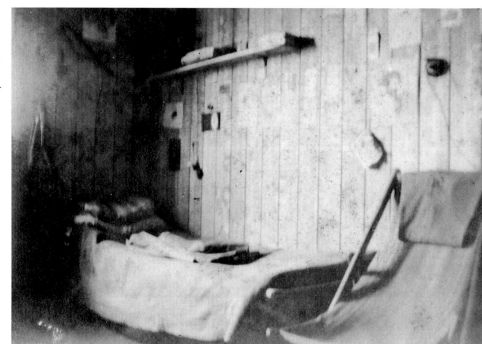

A close-up view of Bebington's artwork and study area. Here his sense of humour shines through. Stationery, art materials and perhaps a letter from home add those small touches which make Army life more bearable. Cadet Bebington was a competent artist: we can only wonder at his subjects of the Dickensian caricature, the young lady dressed perhaps not for taking home to meet mother, and the map on the wall perhaps of France or simply another exercise. A view into a world 100 years past.

Cadet Harold Cooper Bebington was 'Gazetted' (that is, confirmation of his appointment was printed in the London Gazette) on 7 August 1916 as Second Lieutenant (on probation) to the West Lancashire Brigade of the Royal Field Artillery effective from 8t August 1916. In this picture with two brother officers in full service dress, Bebington (centre) wears his rank on his epaulettes whilst the other two officers wear theirs on the cuffs of their tunics. The penchant for wearing shoulder rank badges started with the Brigade of Guards and became standard practice within the British Army. Many British officers were to fall victim to German snipers through wearing cuff rank badges, being all too different and noticeable from the other ranks they commanded. The shoulder rank badges were known as 'wind-up' tunics. Robert Graves, the war poet, having been attached to the Welsh Regiment where shoulder rank badges were the norm, on return to the more 'traditional' Royal Welsh Fusiliers was to be dressed down by a senior officer and made to purchase a cuff-rank tunic.

Bebington in cricket whites obviously enjoying the benefits of sport together with the ubiquitous cigarette. A happy young officer, blissfully ignorant of what fate has in store for him.

Bettisfield, October 1916

The West Lancashire Brigade of the RFA was a formation of the Territorial Force of the 55th West Lancashire Division, the Division being established in France in November 1915. Many friends in different regiments from the Merseyside and surrounding areas would find themselves serving in this Division on the Western Front. Bettisfield was a satellite camp of the large Oswestry military training area and home to the depot unit (amongst others) of the 55th Division.

The Royal Artillery maintained a presence in Oswestry until the late 1960s, as is no doubt remembered by many a National Serviceman. Some of the remaining barrack huts can still be seen and indeed are still used for events at what is now Oswestry Showground.

Mounted officer of the Royal Regiment of Artillery in what appears to be field service order as a haversack is worn. The vulnerability of both horse and rider to the high-velocity modern round is painfully obvious to all.

'An elf and a mushroom.' A wonderfully-posed picture of Second Lieutenant Bebington who has now taken to smoking a pipe. J. R. R. Tolkien's experiences in another Lancashire regiment inspired his 'Lord of the Rings' novels; here Bebington is seen in a humorous photograph, just a simple bit of fun.

From the start of the War, the soldier's addiction to tobacco was understood to be linked with morale, plummeting if it ran low. Somehow the soldiers carried on 'whilst they had a Lucifer to light their fag'. Cigarettes of the time had no filter and the tobacco was extremely strong, but when risking life and limb on a daily basis by comparison it was a risk worth taking.

'Charlie on the warpath.' The biggest film star of the age was Charlie Chaplin, sometime resident of a London workhouse; here we see his most famous character the Tramp celebrated by two Artillery officers alongside a young lady who has acquired one of the officer's service caps. One of the officers is of course our Second Lieutenant Bebington holding a cane whose sense of humour again shows through. The young lady seems happy to be in the company of the two officers, but sadly Bebington neglects to inform us as to who she is. Perhaps the 'Lady from Amsterdam' of his artwork?

Just 'Charlie' Bebington in this picture. Perhaps the lady and the other officer of the previous picture were watching in amusement. Bebington seems to relish his role centre stage, but dress regulations for the Royal Artillery fail to make mention of in what type of dress a straw boater is to be worn! Bebington's sense of humour no doubt stood him in good stead with the men he commanded in the battles to come.

'Shopping.' A fellow officer assigned to the 55th Brigade shopping in the Welsh border village of Hanmer. Hanmer, once home to a supporter of Owain Glyndwr and scene of a particularly bloody English Civil war ambush, is a sleepy village not far from Bettisfield. The off-duty officers seem to amuse the well-dressed local ladies (it is noted that none are wearing mourning), the local shop seems to have plenty of items to purchase in its window though by this, the third year of the War, rationing would be making itself felt, the Merchant Navy suffering heavy losses from German submarines. The Royal Artillery officer pictured is immaculately turned out in his service dress (no doubt the result of many hours' work by his personal servant or batman) but wears no evidence of overseas service as yet. This was denoted by inverted chevrons on the sleeve, red for 1914 and blue for each subsequent year. No doubt he and Bebington are enjoying the period of calm before making their way to the Front.

'C.C. Rees.' This smiling young officer is making a lucky two-thumbs-up gesture to the photographer. Charms were popular with the other ranks. The gesture itself is universal as one of good fortune.

'Sunday morning, Hanmer.' A beautiful picture of rural tranquillity in a small village. Women and children walk perhaps to or from Church, but no men to be seen.

'Some Sentry.' Lieutenant Bebington again plays to the camera, his strength of character obvious as in full service dress with cane and a bucket of coal for the stove, he stands guard. His tunic this time is of the cuff-rank type, popular at the beginning of the War but, as has been noted, once in France no longer viewed as suitable in action. Lieutenant Bebington certainly seems wealthy enough to afford a number of service dress tunics.

'Reesy and Bobby.' Two officer colleagues definitely at their ease – hands in pockets and an unusual linked-arms drill movement, perhaps peculiar to the Artillery! Bebington's ability to put his subjects at their ease is all too evident. What would the Colonel have thought if he had found his officers 'skulking'?

'Officer's Mess, Bettisfield.'

'Captain Orrell and C. C. Rees.' Another shot taken behind the 'skulking' shed!

Chapter Three

Harold Bebington and the Doctor

To obtain a position as a potential officer, Harold Cooper Bebington needed to provide a reference from someone with a military connection. Family friend Archibald Gordon Gullan (known as 'A.G.' to Harold), a Lieutenant-Colonel in the RAMC – Territorial Force, signed his Certificate of Moral Character in his capacity as Officer Commanding 1/3 West Lancashire Field Ambulance then at Canterbury in October 1915.

Archibald Gordon Gullan was a Consulting Physician and Surgeon working from 37 Rodney Street in Liverpool (Rodney Street in Liverpool is noted for the number of doctors there and also its Georgian architecture – it is sometimes known as the 'Harley Street of the North'). He had several articles published both in *The Lancet* and *The British Medical Journal*. Born in Swansea in 1871, he lived his early life in Tranmere, Birkenhead, and attended the Birkenhead School before studying at University College Liverpool later specialising in medicine. On the creation of the Territorial Force in 1908 he was appointed Major in the 1st West Lancashire Field Ambulance. He was at one time the Medical Officer to the Liverpool Scottish (a role later filled by two-times Victoria Cross winner Captain Noel Chavasse, son of the Bishop of Liverpool). It was only at the outbreak of the War in 1914 that he transferred to command the 3rd with the rank of Lieutenant-Colonel. This unit served in France as part of the 55th West Lancashire Division, as would later Bebington but in the Divisional Artillery.

The 3rd West Lancashire Field Ambulance left from Southampton for France on 13 January 1916 to become part of the 55th Division. Lieutenant-Colonel Gullan remained with them until the end of July 1916 at which point he was invalided home with severe trench fever (which in 1918 was discovered to be caused by lice). On resuming duty back in England in January 1917, he held various posts in Western Command and eventually became Officer Commanding Queen Mary's Military Hospital, Whalley, Lancashire. In February 1918 he was selected for the post of Officer Commanding the Military Hospital, Gibraltar, returning home late that year.

The newly-commissioned Second Lieutenant Bebington with Lieutenant-Colonel Gullan on the right of the picture in 1916. It is apparent that both are at ease in each other's company, their friendship is one of over seven years' duration, perhaps beginning with the early death of Bebington's father and his medical care.

'A.J., A.G. and Lou.' Lieutenant-Colonel Gullan with his second wife Louisa ('Lou') to the right of the picture, whom he married in 1913 in West Derby.

Another picture of Gullan with the unknown lady 'A.J.'. The intimacy of these photographs and the smiles evident reinforce the family-friend connection. Even the stance might be posed for the camera!

Lieutenant-Colonel Gullan on horseback. This picture was probably taken in France. The horse has seen hard service. Gullan sits his steed with an air of quiet competence, setting a calm example as a capable leader of men. Note as an officer of the Royal Army Medical Corps, although he wears a Sam Browne belt, he is unarmed as per the Geneva Convention.

Another fine mounted picture of Lieutenant-Colonel Gullan, an officer and a gentleman who dedicates his life to the care of others. The horse appears to bear the brand of the Board of Ordnance, denoting its military ownership and is in very well-groomed condition. Two other-rank orderlies wait at a discreet distance as the Lieutenant-Colonel has his picture taken.

The officers of the 1/3 West Lancashire Field Ambulance Unit with Lt. Col. Gullan seated centre front. The officer to his right is not wearing an open officer's tunic but does appear to have cuff rank on display, it being that of a Major. This is perhaps an attempt at a 'combat' uniform, it not being unknown for enemy snipers to treat those giving aid to wounded as fair game. The wealth of experience provided by this group of officers is evident from their faces; sadly it is only to be speculated what suffering that they had to deal with.

Centre stage mounted sits Gullan surrounded by his officers, immediately flanked by his two Majors. Mostly the medics are all men approaching middle age with a wealth of medical knowledge and experience. With so many experienced medical men away at the Front, what effect did this have on the civilian population back in Blighty? In both pictures, the veteran subaltern second from the right (with the prominent moustache!) appears to have acquired a pair of motorcycle gloves for warmth.

A member of the RAMC and a friend of Bebington's from his archive, unfortunately unidentified, but dated 3 November 1915. Perhaps one of Gullan's command undergoing training at Canterbury.

Chapter Four

In Flanders, 1917

Second Lieutenant Harold Cooper Bebington embarked for France on 27 March 1917 to join the Royal Field Artillery brigades of the 55th West Lancashire Division in the Ypres Salient in Flanders where the Division had been located since the end of 1916.

In France ahead of him was Major Knox (the Officer Commanding the RA cadet training school) who, either by choice or necessity, had found himself at the Front. He was by this time 54 years old. Severely wounded in action and returned to England, he committed suicide on St. George's Day (23 April) 1917 and is buried at the Greenwich Cemetery, London.

The training back in England had been to make Bebington a competent officer, now he had to learn skills within the Division upon which his very survival depended. Gas school, including the practicalities of putting a gas mask onto a panicking horse – no horse, no mobility. Camouflage school – by 1917 camouflage was becoming an art form, and a new RFA officer had to learn how to disguise his guns, though once in action this was often a forlorn hope as blast from the weapon destroyed any imitation foliage and suchlike. Being a man wise to the ways of the world from his commercial background, Bebington would already have learned as to what kit was viable for the task. At no point is he ever seen with a sword; dress regulations may have required it, but for a front-line officer it was just a waste of money, something left with the baggage train and something for a light-fingered Tommy to purloin!

Bebington would also have attended schooling in the use of the .455 calibre pistol, usually the large Webley revolver. An officer could buy his own handgun, which had to take service ammunition, although if ever he had to draw his weapon in anger, his gun position would have been overrun and his military career at an end either as a casualty or as a prisoner of war.

Having attended all relevant training courses, Bebington would then be attached as a supernumerary to a battery on a 'quiet' front, there to become acquainted with active service and its stresses and strains imposed on an officer by both the enemy and the ways of that well-intentioned but occasionally wayward creature, the British private soldier! His experience in man-management in civilian life within the family business no doubt enabled him to settle in to his Brigade where he was in command of a section of two 18-pounder field guns with their horses and twenty men.

Much could still go wrong with the equipment supplied to the British gunner in 1917: fuzes could be unreliable and sometimes plain dangerous! German artillery was both efficient and well served by competent gunners, at least as professional as its British counterparts. The 55th Division was under almost constant German artillery fire whilst it was in the salient.

Passchendaele

During June and July 1917 preparations by the British for a massive offensive in the Ypres Salient were in hand. Roads were repaired, vast quantities of ammunition, stores and equipment assembled. The opposing German Fourth Army cannot have failed to notice this work, particularly as they frequently enjoyed the advantage of being in command of the high ground and so enjoyed better observation with the consequence of counter-battery fire. The Germans had also been making great advances in the use of aircraft in a ground-attack role, a most unpleasant experience for the attacking British infantry and its hardworking brothers in the Royal Artillery.

The artillery bombardment which was to be the prelude to the Third Battle of Ypres (known as Passchendaele) started in earnest on 12 June 1917. The 55th Division had thirty-two brigades of artillery available (although these were understrength), amounting to 768 guns

Bebington's guns were involved in the preparatory bombardment as a prelude to the infantry assault on Pilckem Ridge, his guns firing at the slower rate of four rounds per minute (twenty was possible with the QF field gun) in order to preserve their barrels. The Field Artillery was instructed to advance with the infantry to provide covering support fire where possible.

Due to the very wet weather conditions which have become synonymous with the Western Front, and the fact that the British commander Field Marshal Sir Douglas Haig did not receive approval for the Flanders operation from the War Cabinet and Prime Minister Lloyd George in London until 25 July, the full attack did not commence until the 31st. German counter-battery fire was savage, having the advantage of better observation, and the British Royal Flying Corps was unable to establish air superiority until late in the day. With the shelling and the disruption to field telephone cables laid by the Royal Engineers Signals Service (the Signals Corps was not formed until after the Great War), communications at the Front were often reduced to the use of carrier pigeons.

Broken Spur

In the battle for Pilckem Ridge, the 55th Division suffered 168 officer and 3,384 other-rank casualties. Amongst the officer casualties was Second Lieutenant Harold Cooper Bebington, who was gassed and wounded in the leg at the very start of the battle. He had survived just over four months at the Front since his arrival in France. The spurs which he was wearing at the time of his wounding and which have been seen in the photographs of his training were broken. These are now in the possession of the authors, together with other items of his military service he kept as mementos.

The broken set of spurs and hip flask.

He would have first received medical attention at a Regimental Aid Post based just behind the front line manned by a RAMC medical officer, generally a captain or a lieutenant, assisted by a sergeant, orderlies and stretcher-bearers. The officer would assess the patient, administering morphine to those in pain and giving emergency treatment where possible (Captain Noel Chavasse VC performed such a role). The assessment would identify those who could be saved and those who could not. With a serious leg wound, Bebington was then sent further back behind the lines by stretcher to a static Advanced Dressing Station. This would have been run by a field ambulance section of the RAMC; Bebington's friend Lieutenant-Colonel Gullan was in command of such a field ambulance, but by this time he was back in England. The level of treatment available here by 1917 included operations on urgent cases. Further treatment was provided at a Casualty Clearing Station out of range of enemy artillery, from where motor ambulances might be available to carry wounded men to fixed hospitals located in the rear. At the hospital, those badly-wounded soldiers who were fit enough to travel were placed aboard an ambulance train for the further journey back to Britain. Many men prayed for a serious but not fatal wound which would require them to be sent for treatment back home far away from the front line – this was known as a 'Blighty' wound.

Bebington's wound was serious enough to require treatment back in the UK, he had received a 'Blighty' and was to be absent from the Front until 1918 when he would return in a new form of warfare.

Chapter Five

Plymouth and Convalescence

Back in hospital in Britain, officers and other ranks were separated for their medical treatment. Officers were allowed to wear their service dress with a blue brassard (armband) denoting their wounded status, whilst other ranks wore 'hospital blues' consisting of a royal blue jacket and trousers, red tie and white shirt with the service cap of their home regiment.

The picture above shows recuperating soldiers wearing the OR uniform. They are from different regiments as their cap badges show, including the Royal Artillery, at a military hospital in Cheshire together with some of their Red Cross nurses. Bebington was sent to the Southern Military Hospital, Devonport in Plymouth for officers. He also had his camera and took photographs of his fellow patients and the nursing staff.

'Nurses.' The nurse sitting down is a Sister in the Queen Alexandra's Imperial Military Nursing Service Reserve (QAIMNS(R)).

'Basil Wood, 2nd Lieutenant RFA.' Believed to be from South Nutfield in Surrey.

'Dicky and Oswald.'

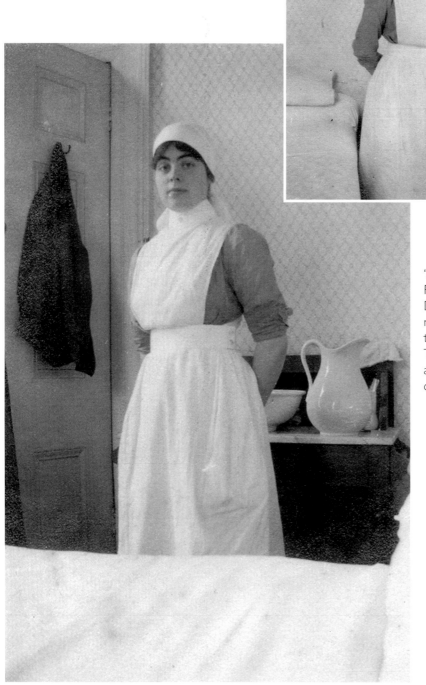

'Robin.' These pictures of Robin, a Voluntary Aid Detachment (VAD) nursing volunteer, are taken in Bebington's room. The room, although basic and for two people, looks clean and tidy.

'Fritz and the Count.' In this picture it is clear that Bebington has not lost his sense of humour despite being wounded. Plymouth Harbour can be seen in the background.

'Two of us.' Bebington on the mend and no doubt buoyed up by a visit from his mother, Jessie. Perhaps she is holding a gift for him in that box! The swagger stick from his training pictures has been replaced by a more functional walking stick to support his wounded leg.

'The Photographer, Plymouth.' Note the single wound stripe evident on Bebington's left sleeve – these were made of brass and pinned through the tunic sleeve. On his right sleeve he wears a brassard indicating his wounded status. He still needs a stick to give support to his injured leg.

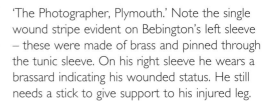

Following a period in the hospital, Bebington is staying at a nearby house located at 59 Durnford Street. From the expression on his face he is still in some pain and still requires the use of a stick.

'Robin and Patient.' The patient is Oswald who was seen sitting out of doors in a previous picture, but still in a dressing gown rather than in uniform as for his colleagues, possibly indicating a more recent arrival to the hospital and hence at an earlier stage of treatment.

Ready this time! The expression of pain on his face is masked. The brassard on his right arm can be clearly seen. Bebington is now ready to return to duty. A final photograph taken in Plymouth before his departure.

'Sister Pile and Mr Hull.' Sister Pile was in charge of the outlying Officer's Hospital in which Bebington was a convalescent. She had arrived from Australia and took up her duties in Plymouth in May 1917, only a few months before Bebington arrived at the hospital for treatment.

'Sister Pile.' She is wearing the uniform of the QAIMNS(R) and a badge on her right breast as a commissioned nurse. This badge was instituted in 1907 and awarded until 1950 and consists of a prominent 'R' surmounted by the King's crown. At the end of the Great War on her demobilisation, she embarked for Melbourne on 21 May 1919 and hence to her home in Adelaide, her duty done and with many officers such as Bebington no doubt eternally grateful.

Chapter Six

New Postings

Catterick

After a period of convalescence in Plymouth, Bebington's next posting was to Catterick in Yorkshire. It appears that as part of his recuperation he was involved in passing on his relevant knowledge to new drafts of gunners, casualties being high for this arm of the Service. Coupled with this was a promotion on 8 February 1918 to full Lieutenant.

Fellow officers at Catterick.

New friends. Note the trouser turn-ups!

A colder day in the north of England. The coats in this picture include the British Warm on the officer on the right and a Burberry raincoat to the left.

Bebington's barrack room. His collection of art seems to have grown, making the otherwise sparsely-furnished room appear very homely.

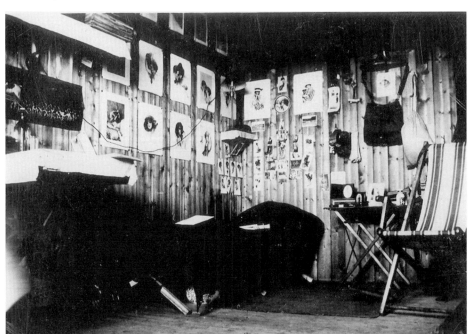

Sergeant Major, Royal Artillery.

Back to Bettisfield – April, 1918

Another transfer and Lieutenant Bebington's training for a new role in the Royal Regiment of Artillery commences. In 1914 the Army possessed little in the way of anti-aircraft defensive artillery. The 13-pounder and 18-pounder guns were adapted with varying degrees of success, but by 1916 the 3in QF anti-aircraft gun had finally reached the Royal Artillery in significant numbers, and it was in this new form of gunnery that Bebington was to see combat again.

At the commencement of the Great War in 1914, powered aircraft had only been available since the Wright brothers in 1906 so their use in warfare was novel. Airships or Zeppelins had been available since the turn of the twentieth century, but the shooting down of either from the sky by anti-aircraft gun was a more recent development, with serious research only beginning in 1910.

'Helios.' Refresher training on signalling.

'The QF's.' The officers in training selected to command the new anti-aircraft guns.

The Quick Firers with hats! Lt Bebington, seated on the ground, displays on his sleeves the wound stripe and one year's service chevron, which are not worn by the others, indicating that he is the only one with combat experience.

'Robbie.' A holder of the Military Cross holder, as seen from the medal ribbon worn above the left pocket of his tunic. The Military Cross was instituted in December 1914 for award to commissioned officers for acts of gallantry. It wasn't until March 1916 that a similar medal called the Military Medal was instituted for Other Ranks.

'Bebbie.' The photographer with a new set of spurs.

An unusual grouping of Royal Field Artillery personnel outside their canteen comprising six officers and one Other Rank, all at their leisure in varying states of uniform undress with four with their hands in their pockets including the OR, an indication perhaps of the close bonds within this particular unit. The officer at the extreme right has one wound stripe and what appears to be the ribbon of the Military Cross on his tunic.

Lieutenant Bebington and friends. Looking very relaxed and recovered after his wounding some nine months ago, and enjoying his new role.

A Royal Artillery officer with a different type of mount!

The Anti-Aircraft Guns

With the Kaiser offensive of 1918 running out of steam, by late April 1918 the danger of a German breakthrough had passed. The German Army had suffered heavy casualties and now occupied ground which would prove impossible to hold with their depleted units. In August 1918, the Allies began a counter-offensive, using new artillery techniques. Lieutenant Bebington returned to the Western Front in June 1918 with his AA guns and crews in preparation to take part in this offensive. It is believed that only 102 such lorry-mounted 3in anti-aircraft guns were available on the Front at this time, so he was operating very much at the cutting-edge of modern military technology and as one of an elite few. In the turmoil of the Allied advance against the new German lines, Bebington's mobile guns must have raised the morale of the infantry, and their rate of fire and weight of shell would have made them a useful asset.

Lieutenant Bebington survived his second tour of duty at the Front unscathed and was 'in at the kill' on Armistice Day, 11 November 1918. He and his gun crews went on to serve in the Army of Occupation in Cologne, taking pictures of the great Cathedral there as well as the devastation of the Somme battlefields as he passed through. He returned home with his camera to the Wirral on demobilisation in March 1919. His military service in the Great War was at an end.

As the War progressed ordnance factories in Britain started producing more of these 3in guns. Initially anti-aircraft targeting was at best educated guesswork, but Lt Bebington would have had to use a high degree of mathematical ability to enable his section of guns to be effective, especially in the use of the two-piece Wilson Dalby predictor, which demanded a better-educated type of soldier and a more modern 'thinking' type of officer. Indications are that Bebington was such an officer, both from his selection for this new Artillery role and, as his photographs show from their quality, his technically-inquisitive nature.

A photograph taken surreptitiously, apparently from behind a wall, of a 3in anti-aircraft gun and its detachment prior to firing. The guns fired a shell weighing 16lbs to an effective ceiling of 16,000 feet, and had a practical rate of fire of 16–18 rounds per minute. This photograph should not exist as this gun was covered by the Official Secrets Act at this time. Bebington risked a court martial in taking these photographs. By this later stage of the War, the Germans were making great use of aircraft in a ground-attack role, as well as heavy bombers raiding London. This was the British response. The gun crew are wearing light-coloured fatigue jackets, the AA gun being on a fixed mounting as would have been standard to defend static targets such as cities. It could also be mounted on a lorry, providing the earliest example of self-propelled firepower in the Royal Artillery, and which the photographer was to command.

The target for training is . . .

Chapter Seven

They Also Served

Harold Cooper Bebington in the family business of Thomas Peate and Company (which would survive the ups and downs of the 1920s and 1930s to continue into the 1960s as H. C. Bebington and Company) employed numerous local people at its offices, warehouse and smoke house. The façade of the original offices of the Company at that time at 14–16 Richmond Street in Whitechapel, Liverpool, can still be seen today although the lower floor now houses an electronic gaming emporium. He kept a pictorial archive of those employees and his friends as they went off to serve their country in the early years of the Great War, many of whom are identified in his albums but unfortunately some are not, however all their pictures are shown here. Some progressed from the ranks to commissions, three won awards for bravery and two did not return.

At the outbreak of war in 1914 and in its first year many of Bebington's colleagues volunteered to join the Colours, whilst some were existing Territorial Force (TF) members many in the 10th Battalion of the Kings Liverpool Regiment, the famed Liverpool Scottish. Many of these TF members would soon find themselves in France as part of the BEF.

The Liverpool Scottish

The Liverpool Scottish was raised during the Boer War and a small contingent served in the later stages of that campaign. Unlike the 8th Battalion of the King's Liverpool Regiment (the Liverpool Irish) which was recruited from the blue-collar working class (dockers in particular for the Irish contingent), the Liverpool Scottish battalion enjoyed a somewhat higher social status with many skilled tradesmen serving in its ranks. It was a kilted regiment, perhaps not the most practical garment for trench warfare, the pleats being hard to get dry and the perfect breeding-ground for lice. With the introduction of gas warfare in 1915 and the blister agent nature of some of the gas types utilised, this led to the introduction of gas bloomers to the kilted regiments, now a much sought-after item amongst militaria collectors!

A Liverpool Scottish corporal, the crossed-flags arm badge indicating a signaller. The attraction of the TF to the ordinary man before the was the two-week annual camp. In the day before paid holidays, it offered a break in routine, the opportunity to learn new skills and to gain an improved social status as rank was acquired. The TF was raised and organised by its County Territorial association which was sometimes at loggerheads with the regular military establishment; frequently different patterns of webbing were purchased due to cost considerations rather than the standard 1908 pattern, but of a type which had less ammunition-carrying capacity and so needed replacement. The obsolescent long Lee-Enfield rifle was also much in evidence using an earlier type of cartridge than the later Short Magazine Lee-Enfield (SMLE). The cartridges were not interchangeable; if the SMLE round was used in the older weapon it could cause it to jam or burst, obviously not a desirable situation for either the gun or its user!

When raised in 1908 the TF was a home defence force not required to fight overseas, though most did volunteer for overseas service (or Imperial Service). Field Marshall Kitchener was uncertain of the overall quality of the Territorials, which led to the raising of the Kitchener 'New Army' divisions designated K1, K2 etc. In time he was to be proved wrong as some of the finest divisions of the First World War were Territorials, including the 51st Highland Division and the 55th West Lancashire Division in which the Liverpool Scottish were to serve until the war's end.

Three battalions of the Liverpool Scottish were to be raised during the War, designated 1/10, 2/10 and 3/10. Ten thousand men served in the first and second battalions (some 10 per cent of whom died in France and Flanders), the third serving as a depot battalion in Oswestry, never leaving Britain. 1/10 Liverpool Scottish deployed to France in November 1914, later joined by the 2/10, soon gaining a reputation for efficiency. Perhaps their pre-war calibre of recruits and training led to a better type of soldier. They had officers they could trust and in Noel Godfrey Chavasse RAMC (their Medical Officer and son of the Bishop of Liverpool) they had one of only three men in history to win the Victoria Cross twice, his example no doubt providing inspiration. The Liverpool Scottish was regarded as a steady unit suffering high casualties, attacking when ordered and surpassing some regular units for their tenacity in defence.

In addition to their infantry role, the Liverpool Scottish had two officers and 100 men attached to the 3rd West Lancashire Field Ambulance as stretcher-bearers; this unit was commanded by Bebington's good friend Lieutenant-Colonel Gullen.

Charles Ernest Bebington (Charlie) was Harold's elder brother. He was to serve in all three battalions of the Liverpool Scottish, rising to the rank of Lance Corporal. In this picture taken at Park Hall camp in Oswestry, he is a mature man having seen service in France. Perhaps he was in the detachment from the 3/10 Liverpool Scottish which provided a guard detachment for the IRA prisoners held at Fron Goch Camp near Bala known as the IRA University! One thousand six hundred Irish prisoners were fed and accommodated by the British including Michael Collins, one of the finest exponents of irregular warfare in the twentieth century, who used it as a training opportunity for when he was released and the civil war he was to win. Charlie was to finish his war in the Royal Defence Corps.

During his service with the 2/10 Liverpool Scottish, Charlie would no doubt have come across the young Basil Rathbone, then serving as its Intelligence Officer. Rathbone was to win the Military Cross for bravery long before he became a star of the silver screen, best remembered as Sherlock Holmes and as Errol Flynn's adversary in *Captain Blood* and *The Adventures of Robin Hood*.

Whilst Charlie awaited redeployment to the Royal Defence Corps, he may also have come across one Norval Marley who was for a brief period a private in the 3/10 Liverpool Scottish before being found unfit for infantry service and seeing out the war in the Labour Corps. Norval Marley is best remembered as being the father of the reggae star Bob Marley.

John Wyckliffe Simpson, known to his family as 'Wyck', was a clerk with the Royal Insurance Company in Liverpool. His family also lived in the Magazine area close to the Bebington family. He was an only son, involved in the Methodist Church as a Sunday school teacher, and an enthusiastic member of the local sailing club. Embarking for France on 23 January 1915 with the 10th Battalion, he was involved in the fighting around Hooge in June 1915 where the German army used their new invention of flame throwers for the first time. The Liverpool Scottish had twenty-three officers and 519 other ranks (including Wyck) making the attack on 16th June. Only two officers and 140 other ranks came through unscathed; as a fighting unit the Liverpool Scottish were virtually wiped out, although the battalion had started to build its reputation as a capable fighting unit as it displayed dash and élan in the attack. Wyck himself was badly wounded. It was in this battle that Captain Noel Chavasse, their Medical Officer, first came to notice searching ceaselessly for wounded between the lines – he received the Military Cross for his actions. Private F. A. Fyfe, a civilian press photographer by trade wounded early on in the fighting, took illicit photographs of the regiment in action while he lay wounded; one photograph shows a Royal Field Artillery officer observer advancing over a German trench parapet to direct supporting fire from their 18-pounder field guns. Fyfe was amongst those rescued by Chavasse, as indeed may have been Wyck.

After recuperation, Wyck returned to the Front and on 24 October 1916 he was commissioned as a Second Lieutenant in the 9th Battalion of the Kings Liverpool Regiment. In 1917 he was awarded the Military Cross for bravery. *The London Gazette* of 17th July 1917 states:

> 2nd Lt. John Wyckliffe Simpson, L'pool R. For conspicuous gallantry and devotion to duty. He led his platoon with great coolness and ability through the barrage, although it suffered heavy casualties. Finding himself almost without men, he took command of another platoon, and, reorganising, the two attacked again.

From contemporary local newspaper reports, Wyck was popular with his men, noted for his compassion towards the wounded and his bravery under fire. He was soon afterwards to be killed in action on 1 August 1917. He is commemorated on the Menin Gate memorial at Ypres and recorded by the Commonwealth War Graves Commission.

'Pte J.A. Dickinson 3104 F Company Liverpool Scottish. British Expeditionary Force. France.' A friend of Bebington's from Wallasey, Private John Arthur Dickinson, a pre-war Territorial soldier with the Liverpool Scottish, is pictured in full field service marching order. His equipment is not regulation 1908 pattern. The local Territorial association, responsible for equipping such units in their allocated area, have cut costs in purchasing a variation of the 1908 webbing supplied by the Mills Equipment Company, which had only six pouches for ammunition as opposed to ten on the standard regular army set. Things such as this played no small part in undermining Lord Kitchener's view of the

Territorials, as many soldiers would require to have their kit upgraded. Private Dickinson is wearing a cover for his kilt, a small gesture to camouflaging this eye-catching item of dress. His water bottle is of an early pattern with the wide mouth, later done away with to simplify production. He is armed with the obsolescent long Lee-Enfield rifle which used a different cartridge to the later SMLE and so placed a further strain on the hard-pressed Army Ordnance Corps.

Private Dickinson, being a Cheshire man, indicates that the Liverpool Scottish did not limit its recruiting to Liverpool; maybe he felt the pull of a Scottish ancestry. He could have joined any of the Cheshire-based Territorial units and so saved himself a ferry journey! He certainly looks a determined soldier. Sent to France on 1 November 1914, he was just too late to see front-line service and qualify for the 1914 Star medal, although he was awarded the 1914/15 Star. He proves to be a soldier of no mean ability, and is singled out to be commissioned from the ranks on 26 March 1918 as a Second Lieutenant. While it was not uncommon as the War progressed for a commission to be awarded to those from the ranks, normally this led to the newly-promoted officer joining a new regiment, thus avoiding the difficulty of giving orders to those he once served alongside. Dickinson was retained within the Kings Liverpool Regiment but posted to its 25th Battalion. In 1918 during the closing weeks of the War, he was awarded the Military Cross for bravery. This was reported in the *London Gazette* of 15 February 1919:

> 2nd Lt. John Arthur Dickinson, 10th Bn., attd. 25th Bn. L'pool R. (T.F.). On October 2nd, 1918, during the successful attack on Two Tree Farm, south-east of Laventie, for most conspicuous gallantry and skilful leading when in command of a company. During the advance he was wounded, but carried on, capturing and consolidating his objectives. Later in the day he led his company forward in a further advance of over 2,000 yards in pursuit of the fleeing enemy. When zero hour struck he was the first over the parapet, and took his men forward under heavy machine-gun and artillery fire. He did magnificent work.

Dickinson ended the War with the rank of Captain. Though the War marked all who served in some way, especially those who were in combat, it must be wondered how those who had excelled and led men in action perhaps even enjoying their service took to civilian life after the War ended. It is hard to imagine a company commander settling back into civilian life, to be given orders by those who had not his experience. The Empire was a large entity, and it needed policing and administering; maybe some were tempted to go abroad to seek new challenges.

The Liverpool Scottish returned home after the Great War to serve again in the Second World War, though as a training unit providing drafts for the Commandos amongst others. Their kilted dead and prisoners feature in the German propaganda pictures taken after the failed Dieppe raid of 1942. Perhaps their high casualty rate resonated again through Liverpool as it did in the First World War. In passing, the roll of honour of the Liverpool Scottish has more named Jones than Campbell listed on it, perhaps as a result of conscription.

Canada

It must be borne in mind how single-minded our photographer Bebington must have been to maintain his photographic archive relating to those friends, business colleagues and employees of Thomas Peate and Company who served in the Great War. In this sole picture of a colonial soldier, a young Canadian infantryman who no doubt left Liverpool for a new life in Canada, has answered the Old Country's call for help. The young soldier also answers the mystery as to how many Canadian and Anzac troops are recorded on British War memorials; they are remembered in their British place of birth and indeed in their adopted homelands.

This unknown Canadian soldier is wearing the seven-button Canadian-pattern tunic which he would have worn until changed for the British pattern as a more convenient replacement for his original uniform soon to be worn out in the trenches of Northern France. This young soldier may have been amongst those from Canada who in April 1915 were among the first Allied troops to experience the German use of gas. The French colonial troops on the Canadian flank broke and ran but the Canadians, equipped only with their handkerchiefs soaked in various fluids clutched to their faces for protection, held and established a reputation as fighting soldiers of the highest quality, sadly at a cost of some 6,000 casualties.

Initially the Canadians were equipped with the Ross rifle, an attempt by the Canadian government to become self-sufficient in the provision of military equipment. Whilst an effective target weapon (good use was made of it by the Canadian sniper who used telescopic sights to augment its built-in accuracy), the Ross was simply not as robust as the SMLE with which the British and Anzac forces were equipped. By 1916 the Canadians had converted to the SMLE though their Ross bayonet with its short, heavy blade was to outlast its rifle in front-line service as it was found by the troops to be useful as a trench knife!

The Canadian Expeditionary Force (CEF) was to grow from a single division to an army of five divisions and a cavalry brigade. It is estimated that approximately 4,000 Native Americans served in the CEF, many employing their traditional marksmanship skills as snipers. Canadian troops enjoyed a better reputation for discipline than their Anzac comrades, and established a reputation as fighting soldiers second to none.

The Cheshire Regiment

'Colour Sergeant Instructor W. J. Mills. November 9th 1915.' Sergeant William James Mills was a long standing member of the Cheshire Regiment, which was originally raised in 1689. His Territorial experience is indicated by the five stars on his right cuff, each indicating a year of service and that he has reached an acceptable standard of efficiency. The crossed rifles on his left sleeve show that he is a marksman for which extra pay was received. There appears to be a single indiscernible medal ribbon on the tunic. He would have started his military career in the pre-1908 volunteer battalions with their origins in the militia and rifle volunteers of the 1860s when it was feared that war with the France of Napoleon was imminent.

In civilian life, W. J. Mills had been a dock labourer living in Birkenhead, according to the 1911 Census. He gives the air of a man of some responsibility and may have later been employed in a supervisory capacity in one of the Thomas Peate and Company establishments. The Cheshires, being the local regiment with the 4th Battalion based in Birkenhead, went on to serve in the 53rd Welsh Division, seeing service initially at Gallipoli, then in Palestine, fighting the sand, flies and the Ottoman Turks, and liberating Jerusalem in 1917. In 1918 it went to France in response to the Kaiser offensive in the March of that year. However, Sergeant Mills is recorded as an instructor and it is as a trainer of men that he would have made his mark using his fund of military experience to turn civilian recruits into battle-ready soldiers.

Birkenhead (famous for the quality of ships produced at the Cammell Laird shipyard) and the Cheshire Regiment have another claim to Great War fame. The local Member of Parliament Alfred Bigland on receiving a complaint that fit men were being refused army service due to their not being of the then minimum height of 5ft 3in, obtained permission to raise battalions of under-height men (minimum height 5ft). These were to be known as 'Bantam' battalions and, in the face of some opposition from the Army authorities, the 15th and 16th Battalions of the Cheshire Regiment were raised in this way seeing much service on the Western Front. Eventually two divisions of Bantams were raised, the 35th and 40th, seeing service in France until the end of the war. Hence the original Bantams saw much hard fighting, and eventually soldiers of average height joined such units as replacements so that the Bantam battalions eventually in effect became 'ordinary' battalions as regards the height of their men.

Wack the Hussar

'Wack', the nickname of Walker Reid Arthur, was probably Harold Cooper Bebington's best friend. They were born in the same year with Wack's father keeping the Magazine Hotel adjacent to the Bebington's home at Marine Terrace. Wack called Bebington's mother 'Auntie Jess', they would have played together as boys around the Magazine, and when old enough Wack was offered a job and he and Harold worked together in the Bebington family business of Thomas Peate and Company.

Prior to the War Wack was a member of the Denbighshire Hussars Yeomanry, which although Welsh in its origins, had its 'D' Squadron based in Birkenhead in recognition of the large Welsh population in the town at that time. Indeed, the Welsh National Eisteddfod was held there in 1917.

'With all good wishes from Wack Xmas 1914.' Wack in full dress uniform complete with chain-mail epaulettes, the tunic being navy blue in colour.

Wack mounted and in 'field order', horse and soldier both turned out to a high standard. He has now been appointed a lance corporal. The reverse of this postcard shows that it was posted in January 1916 from Fencehouses in Durham to Auntie Jess, Harold Bebington's mother. He says that he has written a long letter to 'H' (Harold) at Maxells in London (at this time Bebington was completing his OTC training at the University of London and staying at Maxells Hotel in the Strand), and that he 'did not think H would get leave so soon. Believe he looks fine in khaki.'

Wack's active service was spent on the Western Front. Whilst cavalry remained mostly mounted awaiting an opportunity to exploit breakthroughs that never came, some companies of dismounted cavalry were formed into composite battalions which saw service in the trenches. Wack was one of these, seeing service with the Royal Welsh Fusiliers.

Wack, by now a sergeant, is pictured in the grounds of his home at the Magazine Hotel – the signs of the strains of war evident in his face. Of note is the grenade badge on his tunic sleeve above the sergeant's stripes – this indicates that he is a qualified 'bomber', an expert in the use of the various hand grenades in service with the British Army for close combat at its most brutal. In his dismounted service, his main specialist weapon would be hurling the Number 36 Mills bomb with a seven-second fuze. The fact that a well-trained cavalry soldier trained in the use of rifle and the 1908 Trooper's Sword (called by some the finest cavalry sword ever made!) was to become an expert on the use of bombs indicates how visceral the fighting had become.

In 1914 the British soldier had been well trained in musketry, the rifle being his prime weapon. Lessons had been learnt from the Boer War and fire and movement was a requisite of a British infantryman. Cavalry had also learnt to use the SMLE as its main weapon and, though smaller than an infantry battalion, a British cavalry regiment could lay down a substantive amount of accurate rifle fire if called on to do so. The army that had these skills had largely been destroyed in 1915. The British soldier hence was trained in those skills deemed relevant to the 'big push', many hours being spent in the 'bullrings' (training areas) learning the use of the bayonet to the detriment of musketry. The conscript army of 1918 was very different to that of 1914.

The bomb, or grenade, was quickly to come to dominate trench warfare at the cost of the troop's shooting skills. Senior officers often made reference to the troops' reliance on the bomb in both the attack and defence roles, the bayonet never being popular as it was too unwieldy in the confines of trenches. The Mills bomb (numbered 5, 23 and finally the number 36) was produced in vast numbers, some 70 million in total, finally being retired from British Army service in 1972.

Wack survived the War, returning to the Wirral. In 1974 at the age of 81 he was living in Brow Cottage next door to his father's former hotel, when he was caught up in a gas explosion which resulted in his home having to be completely demolished. Although injured, he survived, dying of old age some years later, saying much for the toughness of the old soldiers of the Great War. He never married.

After the initial stages of the conflict, the cavalry contingent of the British Army in the Great War saw little service in its traditional role, that of providing the 'eyes and ears' of the rest of the Army. In France three British cavalry divisions were formed, later joined by two Indian Army divisions. Total fatalities for cavalry on the Western Front came to 5,674, a mere fraction of the losses suffered by the infantry.

In Palestine, however, much good work was carried out by cavalry, mostly Yeomanry of the Territorial Force. The wide open spaces gave them the opportunity to exploit their mobility against the Turks, a tough and aggressive opponent. Several traditional charges were made, although the cavalry usually fought in a mounted infantry role.

Also to be mentioned are the Anzac mounted units who served alongside the British and Indian units, quickly gaining a formidable reputation. A traditional cavalry charge was made at the Battle of Beersheba on 31 October 1917 actually riding under the Turkish artillery, finally capturing the town which was vital for the Allies. It can only be wondered what the regular cavalry regiments made of their exploits.

The Royal Naval Division

'Jimmie 16/6/15.' Other than the name of Jimmie, this possible employee of Thomas Peate and Company is unknown. As a port, Liverpool supplied many volunteers for the Royal Navy and Merchant Navy. This picture can perhaps lay claim to being the most unusual in Bebington's archive, not only for it being the only sailor but although he is dressed in full navy rig, Jimmie was destined to serve his war as a soldier!

From his hatband, Jimmie is a member of the Royal Naval Division. In 1914 Winston Churchill, then First Lord of the Admiralty, had the idea to utilise surplus naval personnel as a naval landing force, in battalions named after the naval heroes Howe, Drake, Nelson, Hood, Drake, Benbow, Collingwood and Anson. After a limited amount of training and alongside Royal Marines (mostly reservists) they were despatched as the Royal Naval Division to defend Antwerp in October 1914. Though valiant efforts were made by all concerned, the whole affair proved to be a shambles, many being captured or interned in neutral Holland.

Jimmie may be in full naval uniform, but on land when he fought as a soldier he wore either khaki

drill at Gallipoli or khaki serge on the Western Front. Eventually the Royal Naval Division would be armed with the latest SMLE and the 1908 pattern equipment but initially they were woefully equipped with obsolescent equipment.

From the date on the picture, Jimmie is likely to have taken part in the Gallipoli campaign, the brainchild of Kitchener. Kitchener was concerned over the stalemate developing on the Western Front and sought to win the War by opening up a second front and snatching a victory over the Ottoman Turkish Empire. In this he was ably supported by Winston Churchill in his capacity as First Lord of the Admiralty. The Officer Commanding the Gallipoli force, Sir Ian Hamilton, had first seen active service during the First Boer War and had been present at the Battle of Majuba Hill in 1881 where Boer marksmanship eventually caused the British infantry to break, not an auspicious start for a military career and one from which it was not learned that even the best-trained troops will be defeated if asked to perform duties beyond their capabilities and if not adequately supported by artillery – such was the situation at Gallipoli. Turkish and German artillery, mines and submarines led to the sinking of a number of British and French capital ships and their subsequent withdrawal from Gallipoli to a place of safety. These ships had been providing the heavy artillery for the land forces.

Initially, due to the poor performance of the Turkish army in the Balkan Wars just prior to the Great War, the British High Command had underestimated the fighting ability of the Anatolian peasant who, together with an outstanding military leader in Mustafa Kemal Ataturk, made military defeat for the Allies inevitable. Jimmie would have endured the heat, flies, enemy snipers and assaults made by the Turkish infantry, who as well as modern rifles made use of a range of medieval weaponry in hand-to-hand combat. Boy from Liverpool meets the Crusades!

Eventually, the Russian offensive against the Turks that was designed to coincide with the Gallipoli landings was cancelled due to the defeat of the Turks in the Caucasus, and Jimmie and his comrades were evacuated. The Royal Naval Division was reformed as an Army brigade to become the 63rd Division and was sent to serve on the Western Front. It was to establish a reputation as an outstanding combat division though at a high cost – 1,965 officer casualties and 44,829 other rank casualties, of which 445 officers and 7,102 other ranks killed.

Lord Derby's 'Pals'

'Leslie Weber. Lord Derby's Pals Second Battalion.' This picture of this employee and associate of Bebington, Leslie Weber, who went to France in November 1915 shows the only known Thomas Peate and Company member of a 'Pals' battalion. The Kings Liverpool Regiment battalions of 'Pals' were the 17th, 18th, 19th and 20th; Leslie Weber served with the second of these battalions formed, the 18th. Raised by Lord Derby, the idea was that men from the same area or employer would have a ready-made cohesion and community spirit through their shared origins. The disadvantage to this was the high proportion of casualties imposed on their home localities when these 'Pals' battalions went into action. The Earl of Derby's family crest of an eagle and child was used as their cap badge.

Private Weber was to see service with his comrades in the 30th Division on the Western Front, the Battle of the Somme in July 1916 being a particular ordeal leaving many widows in the Liverpool area. He appears to have had some musical ability as he is wearing the insignia of a drummer on his sleeve, the drum no longer served to relay orders in battle but did at least keep the battalion in step when on the march. The Liverpool Pals battalions were to suffer 20 per cent fatalities in their brief existence, but Leslie Weber survived, ending the War serving in the Labour Corps.

Padre

Rev. John Alexander Patten. Chaplains to the Forces do hold standard officer ranks, rather being referred to as 'Padre'. They do, however, hold nominal military ranks or classes, the lowest being that of Captain (the fourth class). Reverend John Patten started his War as a Captain but by the end of the War had become a Major (the third class) before he resigned his commission in early 1919 to return to civilian pastoral care. This priest of the Army Chaplains Department, a friend of the Bebington family, had ministered from 1910 until 1915 at Seacombe Congregational Church on the Wirral at which time he volunteered to became a Chaplain to the Forces. He was awarded the Military Cross in early 1918 for coolness and pluck in bringing in the wounded

through a heavy barrage. He would no doubt have seen much in the Great War to try his faith.

A total of 4,400 chaplains of different denominations served in the Great War, 179 being killed on active service and many others succumbing to disease. It should be remembered that many of these volunteers were not young men. Anglican priests were instructed not to go nearer to the front lines than Brigade headquarters, but this was often ignored. One Roman Catholic Padre named William Doyle won the Military Cross for inspirational behaviour on the Somme whilst serving with the Royal Dublin Fusiliers, and was later killed at Passchendaele. Unsuccessfull attempts were made to have him made a saint! In France however, priests were not exempt from conscription and could be made to serve in the ranks and not usually in their religious role.

Though most pre-war regular soldiers were made to attend Church parade on a regular basis, they were not known as being particularly religious individuals. As volunteers and conscripts started to swell the ranks, they came with stronger religious affiliations and willingly attended the Church services. Frank Richards, the author of *Old Soldiers Never Die*, was a regular soldier serving with the Royal Welsh Fusiliers and was particularly scathing about the change in attitude of his battalion as the Chapel-attending conscripts started to become numerous; not only did they have strong religious beliefs but they also preferred to drink coffee rather than the rum ration!

The Machine Gun Corps

Although not from Bebington's archive, this relative of one of the authors is Frank Jones from Barrow in Cheshire. He is displaying one wound stripe on his left sleeve indicating that he is a soldier of some experience. Unusually he is carrying a substantial officers'-quality cane. His hat badge shows that he is a member of the Machine Gun Corps, and his shoulder badge indicates an 'I' indicating Machine Gun Corps Infantry.

Initially in the War two heavy machine guns were issued to each infantry battalion, the two types being the Maxim and the Vickers. They both required well-trained crews and also men with mechanical aptitude. These guns became a regimental totem: to lose them was a disgrace as the two guns could each lay down the same volume of fire as thirty riflemen.

The more portable Lewis gun came into service in 1915, allowing the heavier Vickers guns to be concentrated into designated machine gun corps of which there were three types:

Machine Gun Corps Infantry (as shown by the soldier in the photograph)
Machine Gun Corps Cavalry
Motor Machine Gun Service

The latter made use of motorcycle and sidecar combinations initially under the control of the Royal Artillery but coming under the control of the Machine Gun Corps in 1916. Many of its members graduated into the 'Heavy' section of the Machine Gun Corps which would eventually become the Tank Corps.

The Machine Gun Corps depot and training area was established at Belton Park near Grantham. A total of 170,500 officers and men served in the Corps with 62,049 becoming casualties (12,498 being fatalities); to the rest of the Army they became known as the Suicide Club! The Corps was not always popular with front line infantry as their presence invited a prompt and aggressive response from the enemy. However, due to its professionalism and effectiveness the Corps stood out as a combat unit of the highest calibre – it was never a parade-ground unit, being born in war and seeing service on every Front.

This Machine Gun Corps Christmas card from 'Bob' is post stamped Grantham 27th December 1917 whilst he was training at Belton Park. He writes to Annie of Huyton, Liverpool, apologising for the late card 'having been away on Duty'. Hopefully he survived the battles to come in 1918.

The Machine Gun Corps was disbanded as part of post-war economies in 1922 with battalions of infantry performing the same role; the Cheshire Regiment was one such selected for conversion.

Royal Garrison Artillery

'John Herbert Oliver
Joined the Colours February 10th 1915
Entered the Homeland June 8th 1917'

Not all of those who appear in the Bebington archive had the good fortune to survive the War. John Herbert Oliver was a delivery driver with the Company. He, similarly to Bebington, joined the Royal Artillery but served in the Royal Garrison Artillery which was the dismounted branch responsible for heavy, coastal and mountain guns.

The British army employed specialist heavy artillery for coastal defence in places such as Gibraltar, Malta, the Royal Naval bases and of course for defence of the British mainland itself. As an army used to fighting colonial enemies, heavy artillery was an area in which it was sadly lacking. The Boer War of only some fourteen years earlier had initially shown the weakness in this area, only partially corrected by the use of naval guns and gunners. By comparison to the German and Austrian armies the British siege train, as it was known, was puny. The outbreak of war in 1914 saw the Army siege train still equipped with Boer War era guns, but the urgent need for an answer to the German dominance seen in the initial attacks of the War on the Belgian forts led to rapid development in this area of heavy gunnery and especially the use of motor vehicles to facilitate movement. Together with guns of 14in calibre mounted on railway wagons, the Royal Artillery gained parity. The destructive power that the siege train could unleash was devastating, usually inviting a rapid response from the enemy.

138772 Gunner Oliver of 235 Siege Battery went to France in December 1916, having received his training at Rhayder in Wales or at Lydd on the south coast of England. He would have first served on the older guns available eventually firing the 60-pounders or 6in guns, perhaps working his way up to the latest 9.2in howitzers firing a range of shells weighing 290lbs, filled with high explosive or gas, but always at the risk of German counter-battery fire or aerial bombardment.

Bebington's written epitaph of 'Entered the Homeland' is his way of signifying John Herbert Oliver's death in France which occurred at the 1st Royal Naval (Division) Field Ambulance from wounds received in the fighting around Arras on 8 June 1917. Sadly Gunner Oliver's widowed mother back in Liverpool would have received the dreaded telegram within a few days of her eldest son's death. He is buried at Bailleul Road East Cemetery, St. Laurent-Blangy, France and commemorated by the Commonwealth War Graves Commission there.

Chapter Eight

The Other Side of the Wire

Second Lieutenant Bebington, when wounded and gassed in 1917 in the early days of the Battle of Passchendaele battle, had seen front lines that were largely static for years, only limited advances and a competent German army that was able to react to Allied offensives in an extremely organised manner, though always at great cost in lives, usually nullifying any gains made.

A Great War German pioneer. Note the torch attached to the front of the tunic, a rare item for a British soldier, and the long-handled spade typical of these specialist engineer troops. The presentation flowers and the flag in the rifle muzzle (together with the wearing of a covered pickelhaube helmet) mark this as early war – once the casualties mounted enthusiasm waned in Germany. And of course the universal cigarette is to be seen, smoking being endemic to all combatants!

As the War progressed, the Germans adapted their infantry tactics to a high degree through their creation of Storm Troop units specialising in the assault, pioneering the use of flamethrowers, and utilising mortars and artillery specific to their role (including using cut-down captured Russian 76mm field pieces). When the Russian Front collapsed towards the end of 1917, with Russia out of the War more divisions were freed to be used on the Western Front. In March 1918 the Kaiser or 'Michael' offensive was launched causing substantial damage to the British Army, success tempered for the Germans by the size of the captured British stores depots crammed with items that had not been seen in Germany for years; the effect on the German soldiers' morale can be imagined as they had been led to believe that the U-boat offensive was causing starvation in Britain.

This posed picture taken in barracks prior to leaving for the Front indicates the close bond between German NCOs and their enlisted men, it being usual to train soldiers to be capable of taking on duties of ranks above themselves. Due to casualties, NCOs sometimes undertook officers roles. Note the white fatigue dress worn by most soldiers, though some appear to be in a form of denim, perhaps the soldier in full dress being about to mount guard. Beer is in evidence, as are pipes and cigars. The leather pickelhaube helmet worn by the standing soldier in the centre back row and the more mature soldiers (not the ever-younger conscripts of the later War years) dates this picture to before or the early months of the War. The cap on the table appears to be of the mountain troops type derived from the Austrian field cap, a style still worn today.

Pre-war conscription was for two years in the infantry and three years in the artillery and cavalry, giving Germany a large reserve army. Interestingly though, not every male was conscripted; only approximately 50 per cent were called to the colours due to the perceived unreliability of the left-leaning urban working classes and, as ever, the cost!

The 1918 German Kaiser offensive was a major blow to the British; the gains that had been hard won over several years were snatched back by the fast moving German storm troops, but eventually it was brought to a halt of which the 55th West Lancashire Division's stout defence of Givenchy-Festubert is a classic example. The long British offensive back started in August 1918, and the British Army had to relearn the art of open warfare. From June 1918 on his return to the Front, Lieutenant Bebington and his lorry-borne guns providing vital anti-aircraft defence must have been an inspiration to the heavily loaded 'poor bloody infantry' as they advanced towards victory pushing the Germans for ever back. In the end, the British had the technological edge, as typified by Bebington's mobile artillery; the Germans moved at the speed of their infantry which was never to be a deciding factor.

German military graves. The precise number of the German Great War dead is not known due to the loss of files in the Second World War. However, two million is estimated.

Chapter Nine

Bebington and the Gunners – A Farewell to All That

By 1918, the Royal Regiment of Artillery had grown to a strength of 548,780 officers and men, and by the end of the war had lost 48,949 killed in action. Many more, like Lieutenant Bebington, were wounded, some suffering for years after the Great War ended. Additionally, many tens of thousands of horses and mules also gave their lives so that the guns could be moved in and out of action as well as to keep them supplied with munitions and the men with provisions.

The Gunner was to see service on all Fronts. He was to freeze, sweat, moan and groan on every continent be it on guard duty in Ireland, swatting flies in Africa, keeping the North-West Frontier of Indian safe, sinking in the mud of Flanders or ensuring civil obedience in the other far flung corners of Empire. Never has a regimental motto seemed more relevant – UBIQUE (Everywhere).

This picture opposite, taken near the close of hostilities, has been selected by the authors as typical of the 'Other Rank' Gunners whom Lieutenant Bebington would have commanded in France. A Gunner, Lance Bombardier, Bombardier and a Sergeant in 1918 as is indicated by the four service chevrons on the sergeant's sleeve – he also appears to be wearing the ribbon of the Military Medal. They indicate the type of artilleryman who won the War, a redoubtable quartet, all of good stature and strong as they would have to have been to manhandle the artillery pieces of whatever calibre together with their appropriate ammunition. Judging by the setting and the lack of field gear, these Gunners are somewhere behind the lines. By 1917 the carrying of the gas mask was obligatory, though these may have been removed for photographic purposes.

The sergeant is in what became known as 'sports coat and trousers' by wearing what appear to be khaki-drill riding trousers (most popular in warmer climates). This mix-and-match service dress with khaki drill enabled the soldier to dress in a manner most suitable to the climate where he found himself.

Apart from the sergeant, the other three Gunners all wear the 1903 bandoliers, which when fully loaded allowed them to carry fifty rounds of .303 ammunition for the SMLE rifle and their personal

defence. However, only a few such rifles were issued to the artillery, so if the Germans got in amongst the guns there was likely to be a scramble for the rifles! The sergeant would have had access to a .455 calibre revolver.

So much for the men, what of Harold Cooper Bebington? Prior to his military service he had already gained valuable man management skills from his civilian occupation. He already had a photographic hobby, and was keen to record the actions of his wide circle of friends at home and fellow workers in the family business as the Great War engulfed their lives. His sense of humour, his ability to mix with others and to command respect is apparent throughout. As an officer, he would have had to act as censor for his men's letters home and through this gain an in depth knowledge of their domestic situations, even the names of their children. He seems to have been a popular man both with fellow officers and with his charges, but with Gunner casualties running so high, how many letters to relatives did he have to write? Lieutenant Bebington's reference from his Artillery training school described him as sober and reliable; it can't have been easy for him but he must have written humane and sensitive letters to those his fallen men left behind. No doubt his own wounding helped him to empathise. But in no way would Lieutenant Bebington have had the advantage taken of his good nature.

Lieutenant Bebington (on the right of the photograph) and a brother officer relaxing after it was all over. No sign of any field gear, shoes worn by the other officer: a definite peacetime feel. He has served, been wounded, lost comrades and friends alike, gone back and stuck it to the bitter end. Now it is time again for civvy street and business, to soldier no more!

In 1920, Bebington was invited to continue holding his commission in the 1st West Lancashire Brigade of the RFA Territorial Army (as the Territorial Force had become in that year). However, he declined, citing business pressures not allowing him to spare the time he thought was necessary for the role.

One task did remain though. That was to place all his photographs in albums together with the pictures of his friends and colleagues as a tribute and memorial to them all, whether or not they survived and in whatever way they served in the Great War. In the future he may have sat and looked through these albums, with a wry smile at the thought of the older images of these people still living close by or still working with him, or a sad thought of those who had made the ultimate sacrifice.

Harold Cooper Bebington went on to take more photographs, marry in 1925, have a family and in time establish another provisions business under his name of H. C. Bebington and Company, also based in Liverpool. He continued living close to the original Magazine family home for most of the rest of his life, with many of his friends and colleagues also returning to live and work nearby from their service in the Great War. He died in 1978.

This picture of the unveiling of the Wallasey War Memorial in November 1928 shows a large crowd, many being ex-servicemen there to remember fallen comrades, and those families who had lost loved ones. It is certain that Harold Cooper Bebington and his friend Wack are there somewhere in the crowd.

And the memorial as it stands today on the River Mersey waterfront, having survived another world war. The seated soldier to the left wearing the slouch hat is actually a gunner from the Royal Artillery; the slouch hat style he is wearing has been in use by the British Army since the time of the English Civil War.

After the Great War ended, the fund raising for this memorial was slow in forthcoming from the general public, hence it taking ten years from the Armistice before its unveiling. Perhaps this was due to a war-weary public or, as the poet and writer Robert Graves wrote, perhaps the colour khaki was out of fashion, for a while at least.